New Directions® For

A Comprehensive String

JOANNE ERWIN • KATHLEEN HORVATH
ROBERT D. McCASHIN • BRENDA MITCHELL

WITH SUPPLEMENTAL ENSEMBLE MUSIC BY
ELLIOT DEL BORGO AND SOON HEE NEWBOLD

The Story of the CELLO

The full name for this instrument is **violoncello**; violon refers to the family of instruments of which the **cello**, meaning little, was a smaller version. Early makers of the modern cello are Montangana and Stradivarius. The adjustable endpin, adopted in the late nineteenth century, is the last physical improvement of the instrument. The cello performs a tenor function in music, often being given a lyrical melody in symphonic works. It has been played in a variety of music styles, including classical, folk, jazz, and rock. Outstanding examples of music for cello are the *Six Suites for Unaccompanied Cello* by J.S. Bach and concerti by Dvořák, Haydn, and Saint-Saens. The performer who brought the cello to a solo status at the turn of the twentieth century was Pablo Casals, and the performer who has brought it to a greater public awareness is Yo-Yo Ma.

Care and Maintenance of Your Cello

It is very important that you care for your instrument as a valuable possession.
Here are important guidelines for the care of your instrument:

- loosen the hair on the bow when not playing so the stick does not warp

- make sure you take the bow out of the case first and put it in last

- rosin the bow with a few swipes each day you practice

- clean all rosin dust from the surfaces of the instrument, strings, and bow stick with a clean, soft cloth

- make sure the endpin is in and securely tightened anytime you are not playing the instrument

- protect your instrument from extreme temperatures and excessive moisture

You should take your instrument to a string repair specialist for a checkup and have your strings replaced and bow rehaired at least once a year. A well-maintained instrument can last literally hundreds of years. Proper care will also help maintain the value of your instrument.

THE
FJH
MUSIC
COMPANY
INC.
Frank J. Hackinson

Production: Frank J. Hackinson
Production Coordinators: Philip Groeber and Rachel O'Kaine
Cover Design: Terpstra Design, San Francisco
Text Design and Layout: Susan Pinkerton

Illustrations: Michael Schmidt
Engraving: Tempo Music Press, Inc.
Printer: Tempo Music Press, Inc.

Visit us on the web at www.fjhmusic.com
ISBN-13: 978-1-56939-574-5

To be a successful cellist, it is very important to learn proper BODY POSTURE.

Here are the important points for correct body posture:

1. Feet on floor in line with shoulders
2. Make an "I-Beam" with shoulders, spine, and hips
3. Shoulders in line with hips (do not twist)
4. Head in line with spine
5. Sit tall

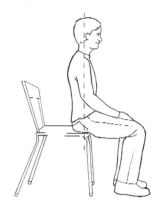

Remember: Correct posture is very important for good health and good playing!

To correctly hold the cello:

1. Sit tall (make an "I-Beam") on edge of chair

2. Cello contacts the floor, knees, and chest

3. Check that the endpin is out far enough so that the C-peg is behind your left ear

4. Give cello a hug to center it in your body

5. Left hand rests on left knee

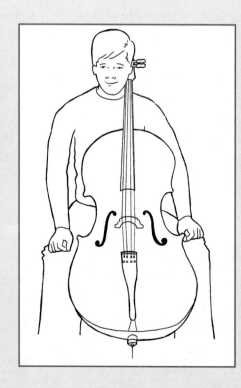

Icons used in *New Directions® For Strings*

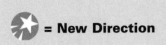 = **New Direction**   = **National Standard**   = **Pencil Game**   = **Review (checkpoint)**

STRING NAMES
C G D A

Plucking Your Strings

1 TUNING TRACK

(X) = thumb spot

 ***Pizzicato*** (*pizz.*) = pluck the strings

2 STRING CYCLE IN 4

C C C C | G G G G | D D D D | A A A A ‖

3 STRING CYCLE IN 3

A A A | D D D | G G G | C C C ‖

 Improvise = to create music

 Making Music with D and A

Use these notes to improvise: D and A

Class Part:

D D D D | A A A A | D D D D | A A D D ‖

(X)

lowest (thick)   highest (thin)

Name your strings.

For each tune: **1. Clap and Count**   **2. Clap and Sing**   **3. *Pizzicato***

4 MARCH IN 4

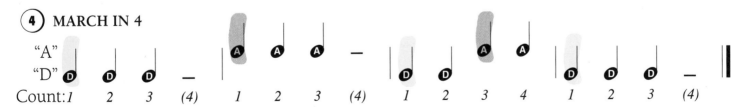

5 WALTZ IN 3

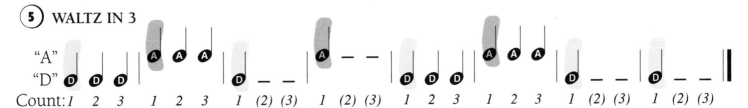

Your First Tunes

Hand Shape

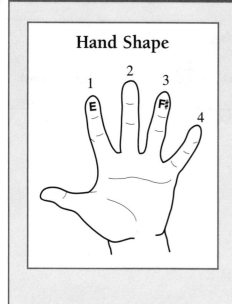

On the Instrument

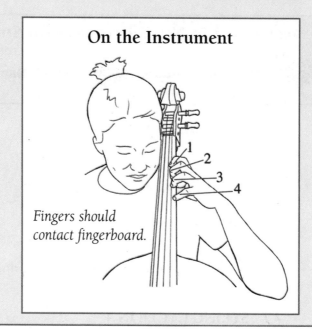

Fingers should contact fingerboard.

Notes:

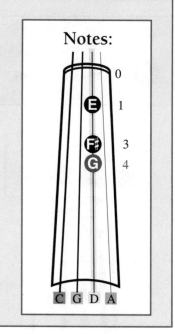

For each tune: **1. Clap and Count**   **2. Clap and Sing**   **3.** *Pizzicato*

6   FINGER PREPARATION ON F♯

F♯   F♯   F♯   - |F♯   F♯   F♯   - |

F♯   F♯   F♯   F♯ |F♯   F♯   F♯   -   ‖

7   FINGER PREPARATION ON E

E   E   E |E   -   - |E   E   E |E   -   - |

E   E   E |E   E   E |E   E   E |E   -   -   ‖

8   FINGER PREPARATION ON F♯, E, AND D

D   E   D   E |D   E   F♯   F♯ |

E   D   E   F♯ |D   D   D   -   ‖

9   HOT CROSS BUNS

F♯   E   D   - |F♯   E   D   - |

D   D   E   E |F♯   E   D   -   ‖

10   MARY HAD A LITTLE LAMB

F♯   E   D   E |F♯   F♯   F♯   - |

E   E   E   - |F♯   F♯   F♯   - |

F♯   E   D   E |F♯   F♯   F♯   F♯ |

E   E   F♯   E |D   -   -   -   ‖

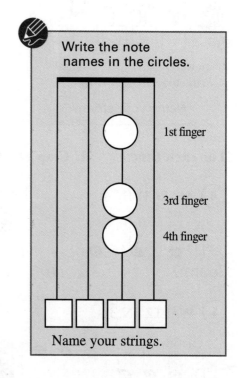

Write the note names in the circles.

1st finger

3rd finger

4th finger

Name your strings.

Continue to review these tunes as you learn the next pages.

Reading/Writing music is a combination of a ladder  and a ruler.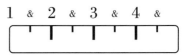

You can:
- Step higher or lower on a ladder
- Measure length with a ruler

Clef =  F = establishes the lines and spaces for your instrument

The cello uses the bass or F clef.

Staff = 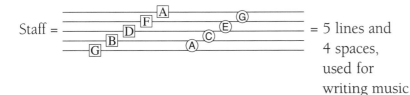 = 5 lines and 4 spaces, used for writing music

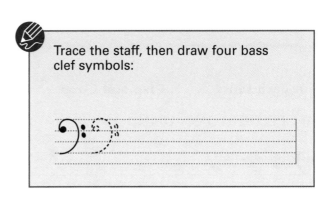

Trace the staff, then draw four bass clef symbols:

NOTE AND REST SYMBOLS

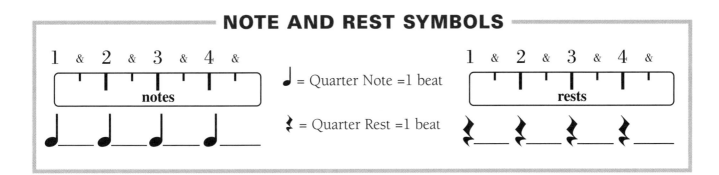

♩ = Quarter Note =1 beat

𝄽 = Quarter Rest =1 beat

This is A    This is D

For each tune: 1. Clap and Count   2. Clap and Sing   3. *Pizzicato*

11 MARCH ON A

12 WALTZ ON D

Write your own composition using quarter notes D and A, and quarter rests.

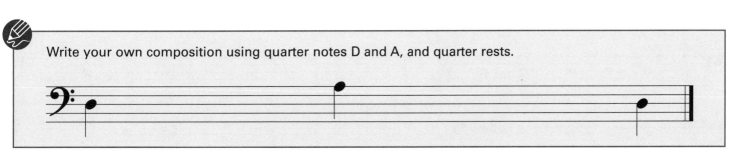

MORE MUSIC SYMBOLS

Time signature – divides notes into groups

Barline – divides the staff into measures

measure   measure

Final Barline

For each tune: 1. Clap and Count   2. Clap and Sing   3. *Pizzicato*

13 PIZZICATO ON D AND A

14 PIZZICATO WALTZ

Your Open Strings

15 STRING CYCLE IN 4

16 STRING CYCLE IN 3

17 THIS OLD MAN

Student part
pizz.

Duet = two parts

English

Teacher or advanced student part

5 Student part

NOTE AND REST SYMBOLS

$\frac{4}{4} = \frac{4}{\text{♩}}$ $\frac{3}{4} = \frac{3}{\text{♩}}$

Cycles with Circles

18 BARCAROLLE — Jacques Offenbach

19 AT PIERROT'S DOOR — French

Complete the measures with ♩, ▬, ♩, 𝄽, using your open string notes or rests (4 beats per measure).
Name and then perform your piece. _____

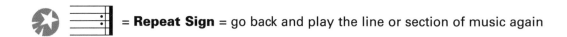

= **Repeat Sign** = go back and play the line or section of music again

20 CHEERLEADING DUET   Duet

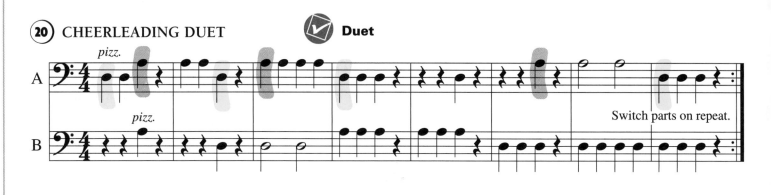

21 SKIP TO MY LOU   American

Name these Symbols

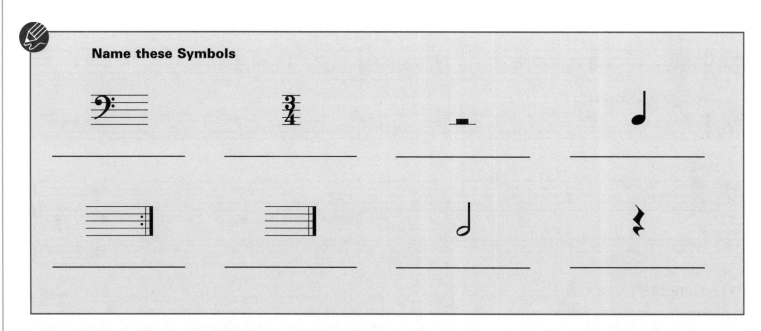

IMPROVISATION LOOP

Take your turn improvising while the class plays *pizz.*

Use these notes to improvise: Use these rhythms to improvise:

Class Part:

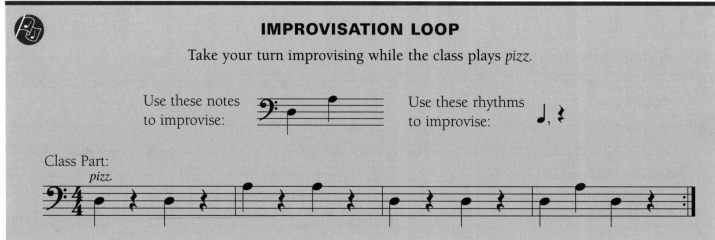

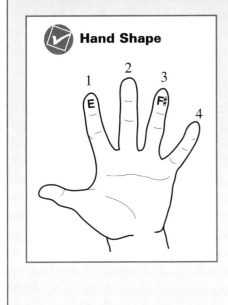

Hand Shape

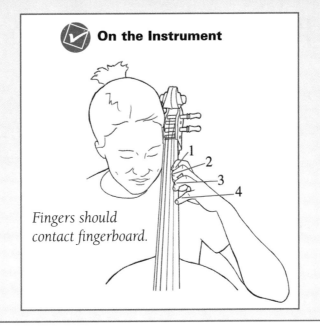

On the Instrument

Fingers should contact fingerboard.

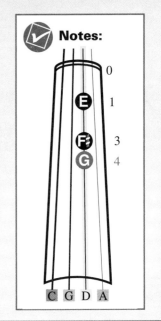

Notes:

MUSIC ALPHABET AND LEDGER LINES

Music Alphabet = the letter names of music notes: A, B, C, D, E, F, G
Once you reach **G,** you begin again with **A.**

Learning F♯, E, and D

Ledger Lines = lines that extend the staff above and below

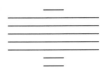

For each tune: 1. Clap and Count   2. Clap and Sing   3. *Pizzicato*

22 PRACTICING F♯

23 PRACTICING E

24 FINGER MIX-UP

25 HOT CROSS BUNS

English

26 MARY HAD A LITTLE LAMB—Memorize this piece.

Sarah J. Hale

Developing Your Left Hand

 Contact Points for the Left Hand:

1. Thumb under the neck, aligned with 2nd finger

2. Hand is in a curved "C" shape

3. Base knuckles are parallel to the neck, wrist straight, and the pads of the fingertips contact the fingerboard

 + = Left-Hand *Pizzicato* (using 4th finger)

4th finger strum

27 D-A-D SONG

28 UP ON THE HOUSETOP

Benjamin R. Hanby

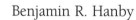

NOTE AND REST SYMBOLS

♪ = Eighth Note = ½ beat

𝄾 = Eighth Rest = ½ beat

♫ = ♩ = 1 beat

𝄾𝄾 = 𝄽 = 1 beat

29 PERPETUAL EIGHTH NOTES

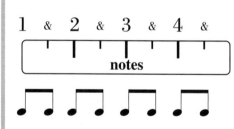

pizz.

1 & 2 & 3 & 4 & 1 & 2 & 3 & 4 (etc.)

30 BARN DANCE

pizz.

1 2 & 3 (4) 1 2 & 3 (4) (etc.)

5

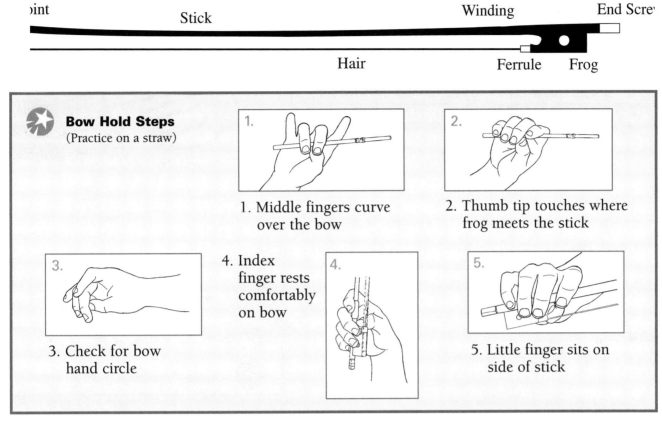

Bow Hold Steps
(Practice on a straw)

1. Middle fingers curve over the bow

2. Thumb tip touches where frog meets the stick

3. Check for bow hand circle

4. Index finger rests comfortably on bow

5. Little finger sits on side of stick

 Arco = to play using the bow. (*Arco* is the Italian word for bow). We always play *arco* unless directions say *pizz.*

⋁ = **Up bow** = moving bow toward frog   ◼ = **Down bow** = moving bow toward tip

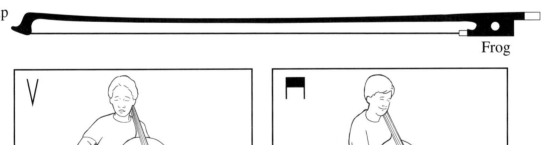

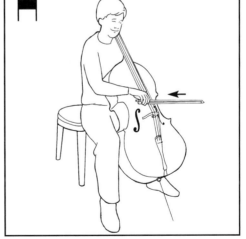

For these Bow Studies: **1. Air bow**   **2. Play on each string**

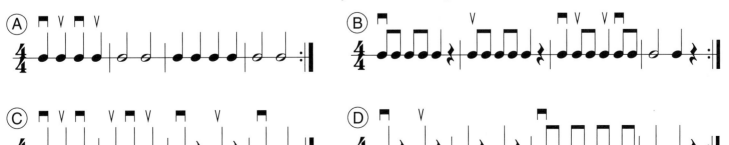

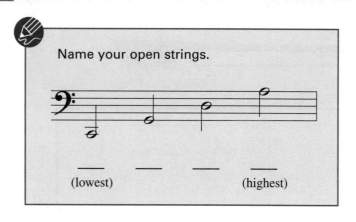

Name your open strings.

___ (lowest) ___ ___ ___ (highest)

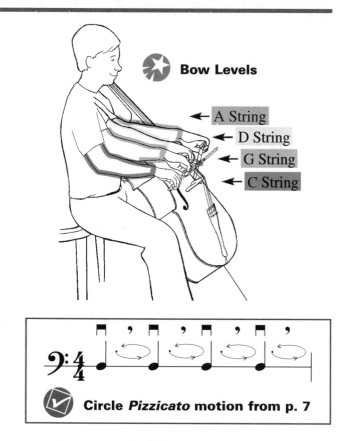

Bow Levels

← A String
← D String
← G String
← C String

♩ = **Bow Retake** = to lift the bow from the string and return to the frog in a circular motion

Circle *Pizzicato* motion from p. 7

For these Bow Studies: 1. Air bow and say bow direction 2. Play on your instrument 3. Memorize one Bow Study

31 TWO AT A TIME   Play two times: first time violas and cellos, second time violins and basses.

32 BOWING ON D

33 BOWING ON G

34 BOWING ON A

35 ARCO ACROBATICS

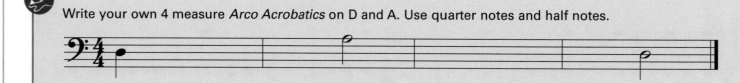

Write your own 4 measure *Arco Acrobatics* on D and A. Use quarter notes and half notes.

Dynamics describes the level of sound, (softer or louder).

p = *piano* = play softly, or f = *forte* = play loudly, with a full tone

With the bow, play your C, G, D, and A strings at a *piano* then **forte** dynamic.

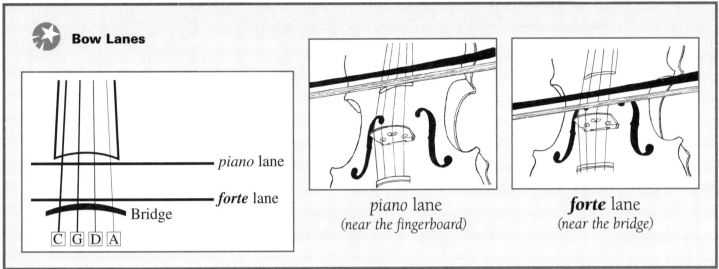

Bow Lanes

piano lane

forte lane

Bridge

C G D A

piano lane
(*near the fingerboard*)

forte lane
(*near the bridge*)

36 DAZZLING D'S AND AMAZING A'S

37 OVER THE WAVES

38 ROUND AND ROUND—ensemble piece

Ensemble piece = music that is not in unison

39 FOUR-STRING MARCH—ensemble piece

SB303VC

Tetrachord = a 4-note pattern
Tetrachords can go
UP (like D, E, F♯, G) or
DOWN (like G, F♯, E, D).

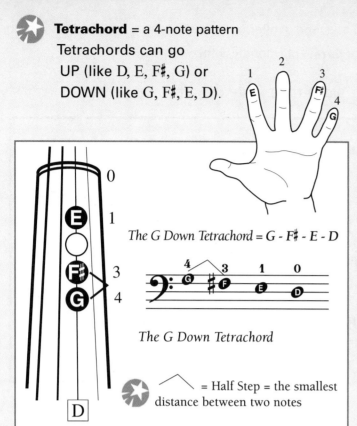

The G Down Tetrachord = G - F♯ - E - D

The G Down Tetrachord

⬧ = Half Step = the smallest distance between two notes

Sing, *pizz.*, then bow these tetrachord melodies.

Sing as your teacher plays the following line, then play.

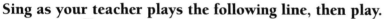

FA is the next Note, then to MI(me), next down is RE(ray), then DO.
Fa Fa Fa Fa Fa Mi Mi Mi Re Re Re Re Re Do

40 OH, GEE DOWN

IMPROVISATION LOOP

Use these notes to improvise:

Use these rhythms to improvise:

Ostinato = repeated pattern of pitches (class part)

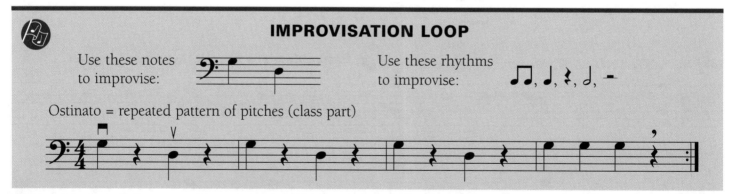

Write the G Down tetrachord. Mark the half step (⬧) and write in the finger numbers.

Name these notes.

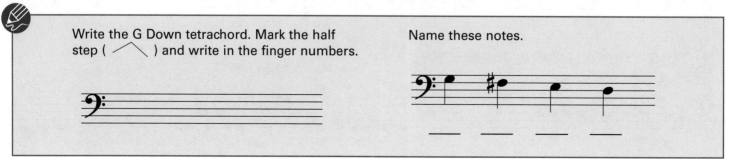

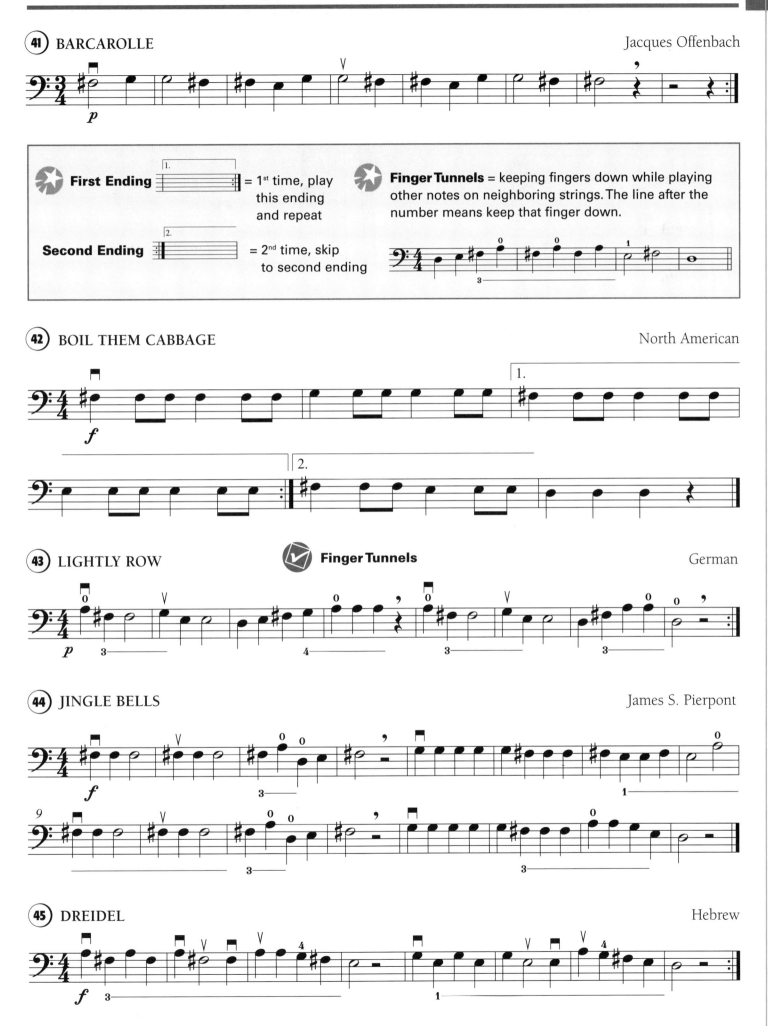

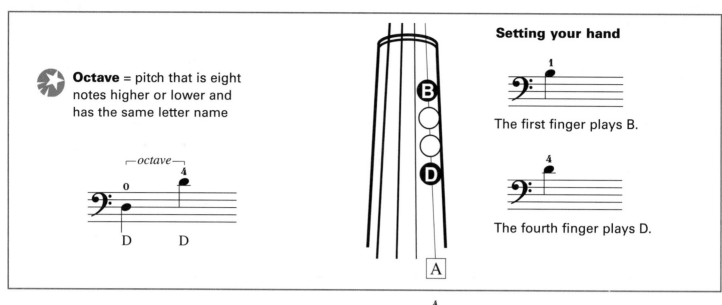

Octave = pitch that is eight notes higher or lower and has the same letter name

Setting your hand

The first finger plays B.

The fourth finger plays D.

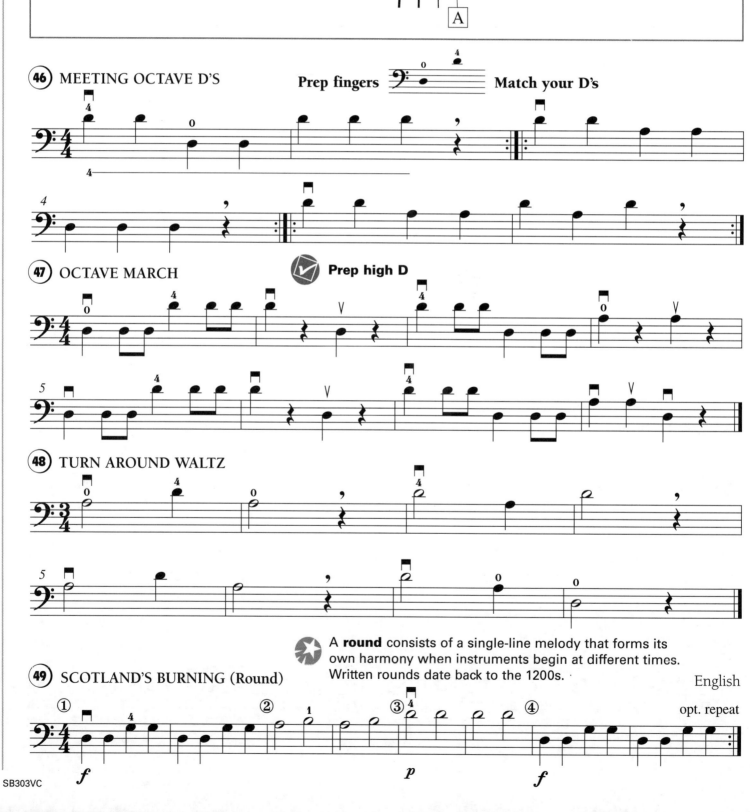

46 MEETING OCTAVE D'S — Prep fingers — Match your D's

47 OCTAVE MARCH — Prep high D

48 TURN AROUND WALTZ

A **round** consists of a single-line melody that forms its own harmony when instruments begin at different times. Written rounds date back to the 1200s.

49 SCOTLAND'S BURNING (Round)

English

opt. repeat

SB303VC

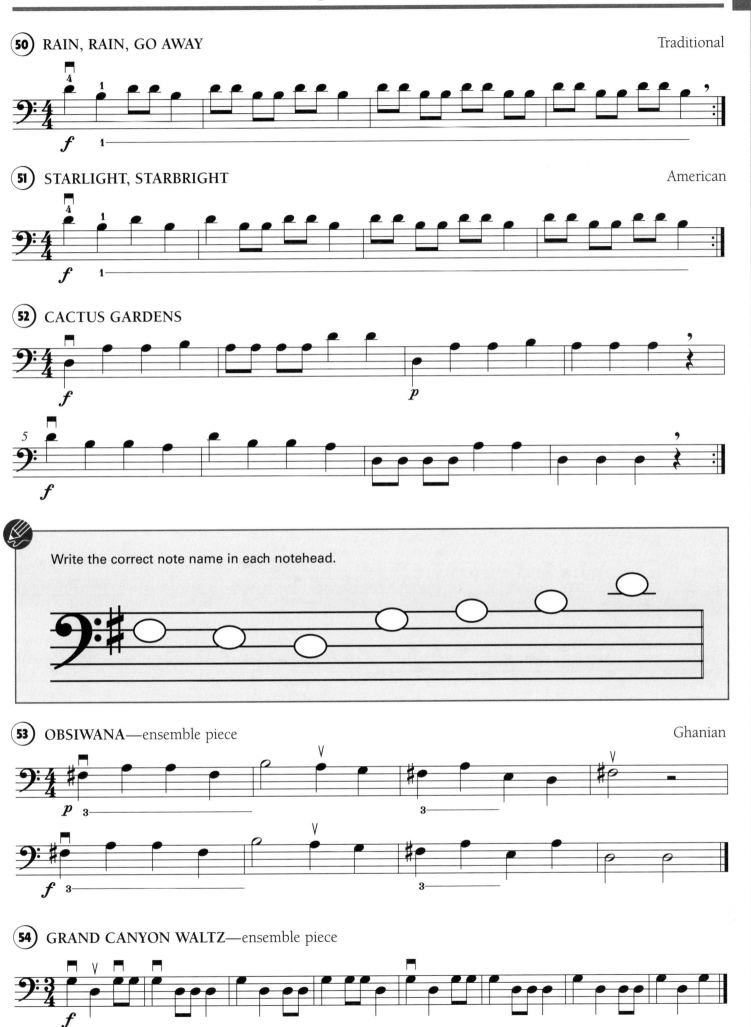

50 RAIN, RAIN, GO AWAY — Traditional

51 STARLIGHT, STARBRIGHT — American

52 CACTUS GARDENS

Write the correct note name in each notehead.

53 OBSIWANA—ensemble piece — Ghanian

54 GRAND CANYON WALTZ—ensemble piece

String Crossing Twisters

Pizzicato each tune before bowing!

With Octave D's in Tune, We Now Add C♯

The D Down Tetrachord = D - C♯ - B - A

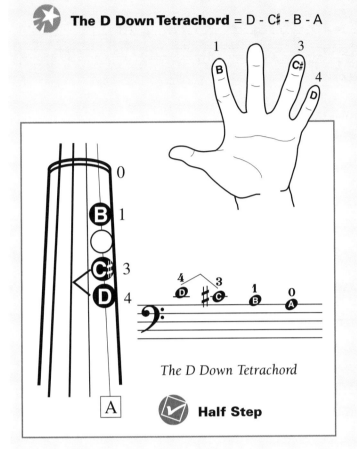

Note Names:	D	C♯	B	A
Finger Numbers:	4	3	1	0
Solfège Syllables:	DO -	TI -	LA -	SO

The D Down Tetrachord

Half Step

Sing, *pizz.*, then bow these tetrachord melodies.

Sing as your teacher plays the following line, then play.

IMPROVISATION LOOP

Use these notes to improvise:

Use these rhythms to improvise:

Ostinato Part:

59) SNOWSHOE DANCE **Prep fingers**

SB303VC

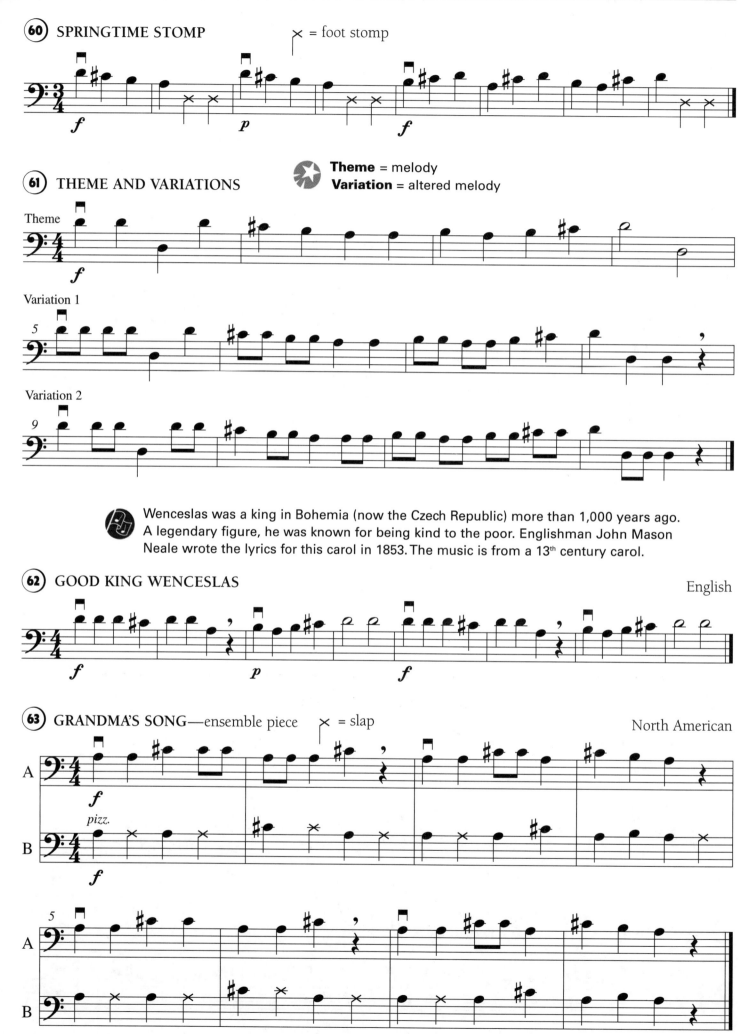

60 SPRINGTIME STOMP ✗ = foot stomp

61 THEME AND VARIATIONS

Theme = melody
Variation = altered melody

Theme

Variation 1

Variation 2

Wenceslas was a king in Bohemia (now the Czech Republic) more than 1,000 years ago. A legendary figure, he was known for being kind to the poor. Englishman John Mason Neale wrote the lyrics for this carol in 1853. The music is from a 13th century carol.

62 GOOD KING WENCESLAS

English

63 GRANDMA'S SONG—ensemble piece ✗ = slap

North American

A

pizz.

B

A

B

Fourth Finger Study Starting on D

Ode to Joy is from Beethoven's *Symphony No. 9.* When it was first performed in 1824, Beethoven was completely deaf. He did not notice the audience's applause at the end of the symphony until it was pointed out to him.

64 ODE TO JOY

Ludwig van Beethoven

65 SPIDER WALK—ensemble piece

66 ARE YOU SLEEPING? (**Round**)—Memorize this piece.

French

67 CHICKEN ON A FENCE POST—ensemble piece   ✗ = slap

North American

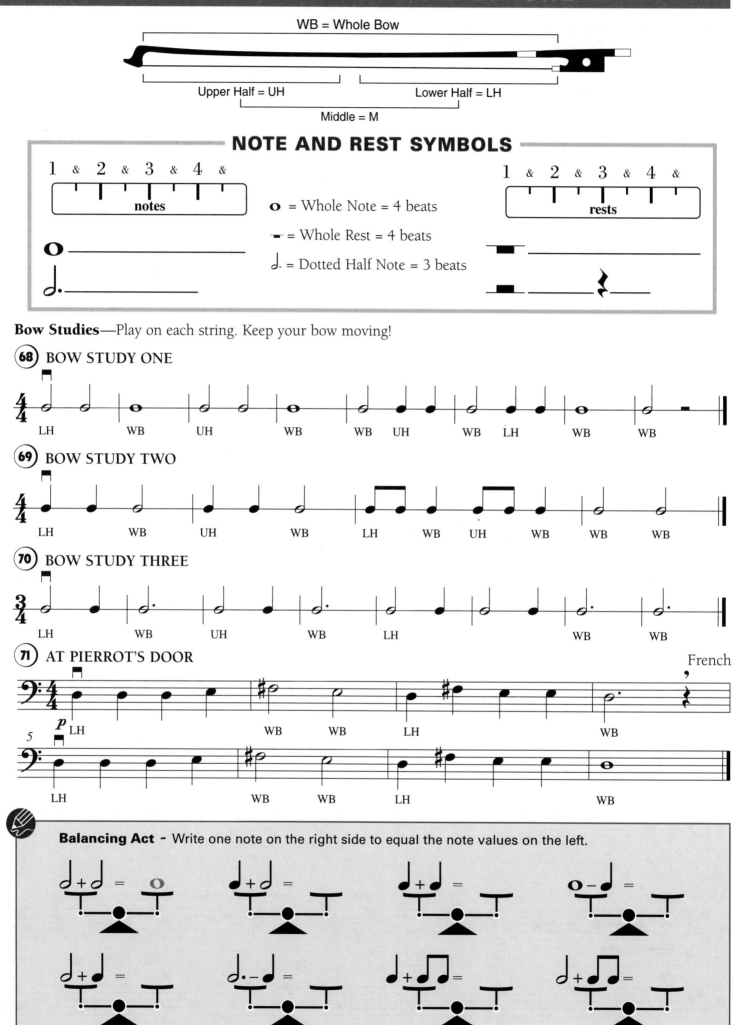

72 GO TELL AUNT RHODY — Bow Lanes — American

73 HOME FROM SCHOOL (*Hui jia qü*) — Chinese

Antonio Vivaldi (1678–1741), an Italian violinist, was known as the "red priest" because of his red hair. Vivaldi was in charge of music at an orphanage for girls in Venice. He wrote over 500 concerti. The piece below is from the concerto, *The Four Seasons.*

74 AUTUMN—ensemble piece — Antonio Vivaldi

Name the tetrachords.

NEW DIRECTION: D Major Scale

 Scale = tetrachord + tetrachord
Scales begin and end on the same letter name.

 Whole step = two half steps

 Key Signature identifies notes
that are raised or lowered.

 = the key signature for D Major

D Scale = D Down Tetrachord + G Down Tetrachord

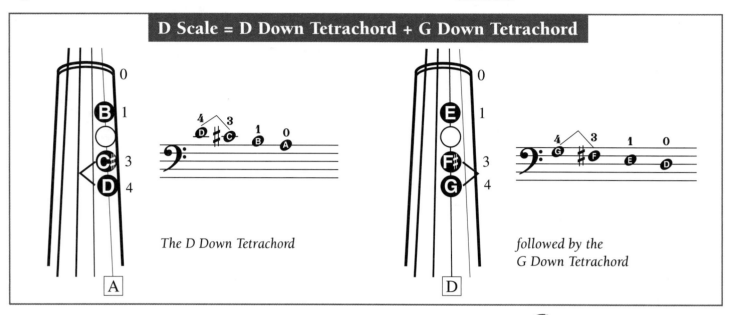

The D Down Tetrachord

*followed by the
G Down Tetrachord*

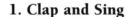 **1. Clap and Sing** **2. Pizz.** **3. Arco**

Note Names:	D	C♯	B	A		G		F♯	E		D
Finger Numbers:	4	3	1	0		4		3	1		0
Solfège Syllables:	Do	Ti	La	La	So	So	Fa	Fa	Mi	Mi	Re	Do

Sing and play up the scale

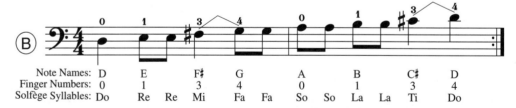

Note Names:	D	E	F♯	G	A	B	C♯	D
Finger Numbers:	0	1	3	4	0	1	3	4
Solfège Syllables:	Do	Re	Re	Mi	Fa	Fa	So	So	La	La	Ti	Do

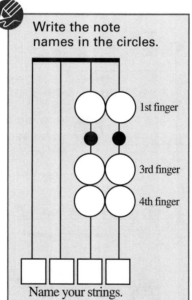
Write the note names in the circles.
1st finger
3rd finger
4th finger
Name your strings.

SCALE STUDIES

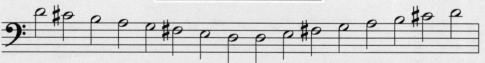

Play the D scale using each of the following bow patterns. (See examples below).
Also, create your own bow patterns.

   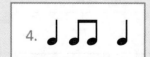 

SB303VC

75 FRENCH FOLK SONG

☑ 𝅗𝅥. = **Dotted Half Note** = 3 beats

French

76 OH! HOW LOVELY IS THE EVENING (Round)

English

opt. repeat

Jacques Offenbach (1819–1880) was a composer of popular music for the theater in France. He played violin and was a virtuoso cellist. "Can Can" was written in 1858 for his operetta, *Orpheus in the Underworld.*

77 CAN CAN—Memorize this piece.

Jacques Offenbach

Switch parts on repeat.

Staccato = stopped bow strokes
Legato = smooth bow strokes

78 JUMPING JACKS—Half class *pizz.*, half class match with staccato stroke.

79 POP! GOES THE WEASEL — English

80 GROUND ROUND

Melody = main tune
Harmony = pitches that accompany the melody

81 TWINKLE, MY EYE—ensemble piece — German
(Harmony)
(Melody)

♩. = **Dotted Quarter Note** = 1½ beats
1 and ½ beats = ♩ + ♪ or ♪ + ♪ + ♪

82 DOTTED QUARTER STUDY: **1. Clap and Count** **2. Clap and Sing** **3. Play**

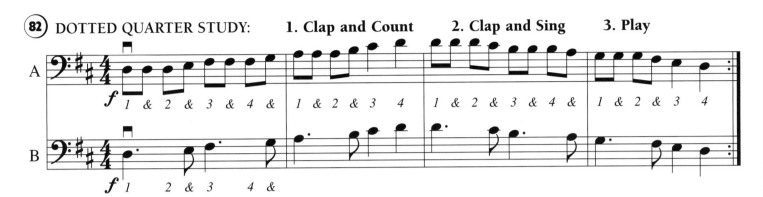

Antonín Dvořák (1841–1904) was from Bohemia, which is now the Czech Republic. He played violin in church and in village bands. He was influenced by spirituals and African-American folk songs while he lived in America from 1892–1895. His Ninth Symphony, "From the New World," included *Goin' Home,* a slave song.

83 GOIN' HOME

Antonín Dvořák

84 LONDON BRIDGE

English

Music Math

1. Two eighth notes = one _____ note, or _____ beat(s).

2. Four eighth notes = one _____ note, or _____ beat(s).

3. A dotted half note = _____ eighth notes, or _____ beat(s).

4. Three beats = _____ eighth notes, or a _____ _____ note.

85 MAY SONG

German

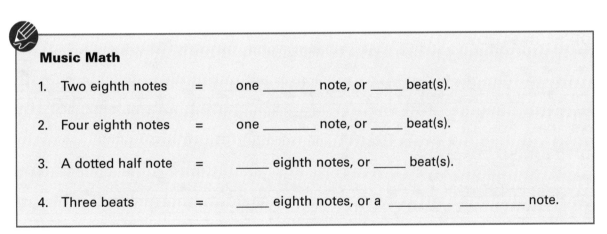

About Bow Division

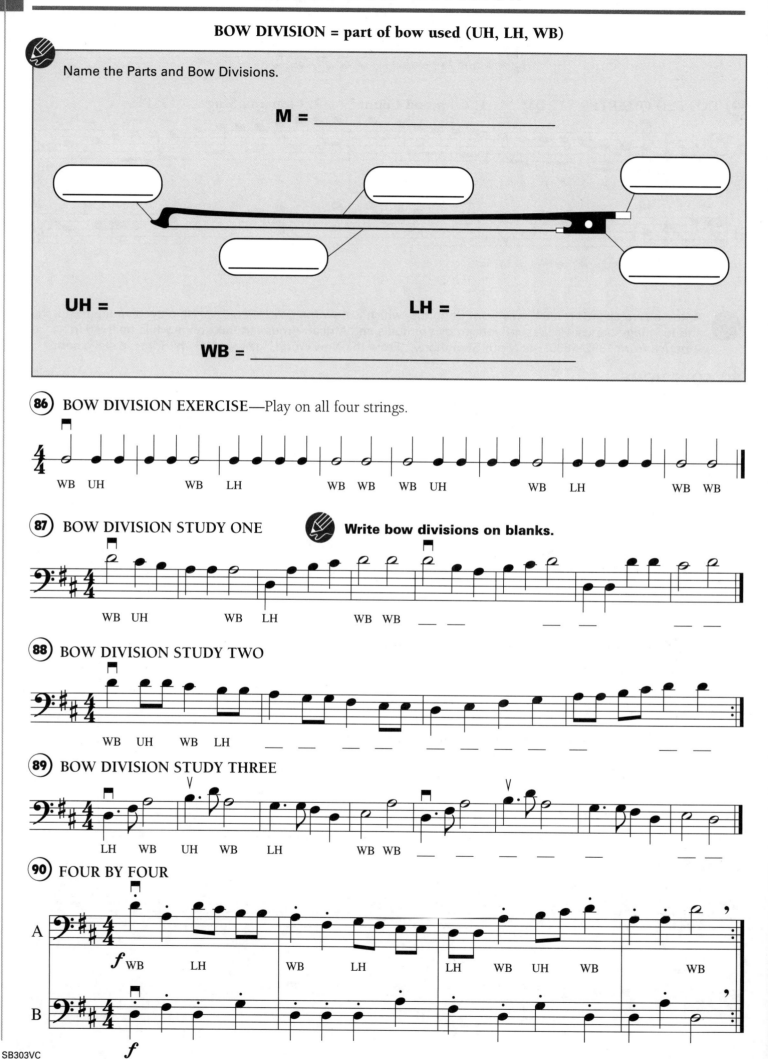

91 STYLES À LA MUSIQUE  **Staccato and Finger Tunnels**

Theme

Variation 1

Variation 2

 Upbeat = note(s) that appears before the first barline. The upbeat is subtracted from the last measure of music.

92 SARASPONDA

Dutch

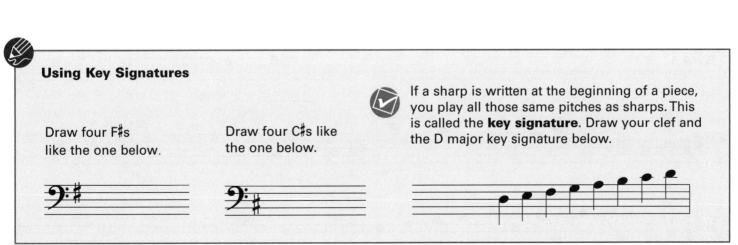

Using Key Signatures

Draw four F♯s like the one below.

Draw four C♯s like the one below.

 If a sharp is written at the beginning of a piece, you play all those same pitches as sharps. This is called the **key signature**. Draw your clef and the D major key signature below.

SB303VC

Good Sound, Big Tone = the correct combination of bow speed, arm weight, and contact point (bow lane)

Crescendo = **Play Louder** = more bow speed or more weight, with bow nearer the bridge:

Diminuendo = **Play Softer** = less bow speed or less weight, with bow nearer the fingerboard:

m = mezzo = medium

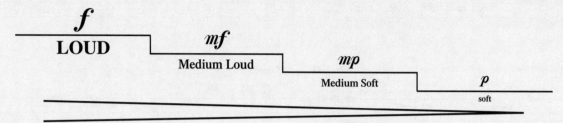

f LOUD
mf Medium Loud
mp Medium Soft
p soft

93 MELODY MYSTERY: **1. Clap and Sing**   **2. Play**   **3. Guess the Tune**

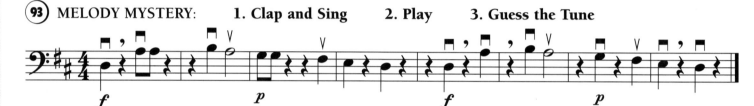

94 COUNTRY GARDENS

English

 f–p = *f* first time, *p* on the repeat

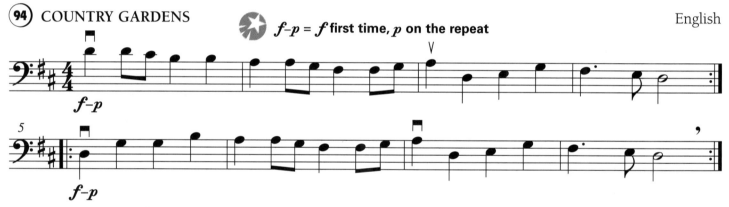

William Billings (1746–1800) was a self-taught composer. He was a friend of revolutionary leaders Paul Revere and Samuel Adams. *Chester* was the unofficial anthem of the American Revolution, along with *Yankee Doodle.*

95 CHESTER

William Billings

Stephen Foster (1826–1864) was an American songwriter. *Oh! Susanna* was the "marching song" for the California Gold Rush of 1849 and was the unofficial theme song for wagon trains going west.

96 OH! SUSANNA — **Upbeat** — Stephen Foster

Johannes Brahms (1833–1897), a German composer, studied cello, piano, and French horn in his youth. He composed large works such as symphonies, as well as chamber music, piano pieces, songs, and choral music. Brahms, J.S. Bach, and Beethoven are known as the "Three B's" of music.

97 LULLABY — Johannes Brahms

98 FIRST CONCERT PIECE—ensemble piece — Elliot Del Borgo

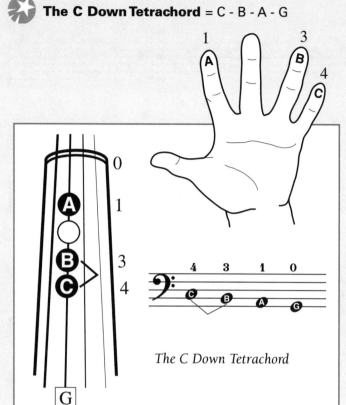

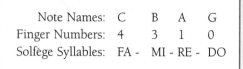

The C Down Tetrachord

Sing, *pizz.*, then bow these tetrachord melodies.

1. Clap and Sing   2. *Pizz.*   3. *Arco*

C Down Town

Waltzin' in C

IMPROVISATION LOOP

Use these notes to improvise:

Use these rhythms to improvise:

Class Part:

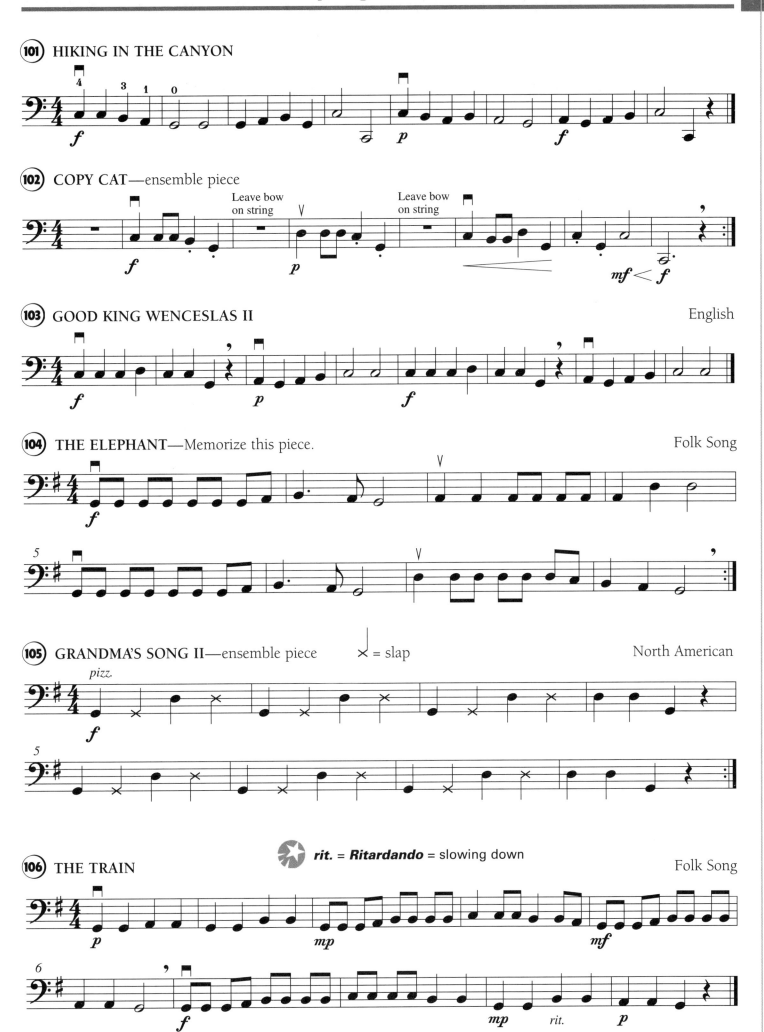

NEW DIRECTION: G Major Scale

= the key signature for G Major

G Scale = G Down Tetrachord + C Down Tetrachord

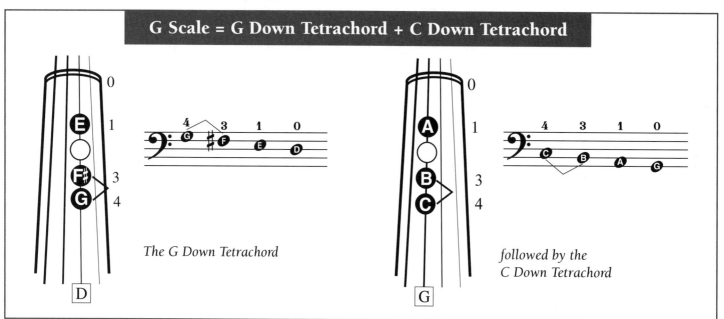

The G Down Tetrachord

followed by the
C Down Tetrachord

1. Clap and Sing **2. Pizz.** **3. Arco**

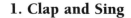

Note Names:	G		F#		E		D		C		B		A		G
Finger Numbers:	4		3		1		0		4		3		1		0
Solfège Syllables:	Do	Do	Ti		La	La	So		Fa		Mi	Mi	Re	Re	Do

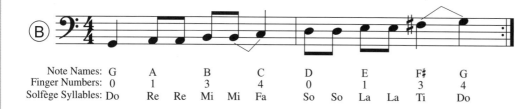

Note Names:	G		A		B		C		D		E		F#		G
Finger Numbers:	0		1		3		4		0		1		3		4
Solfège Syllables:	Do		Re	Re	Mi	Mi	Fa		So	So	La	La	Ti		Do

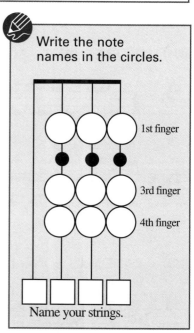

Write the note names in the circles.

1st finger

3rd finger

4th finger

Name your strings.

SCALE STUDIES

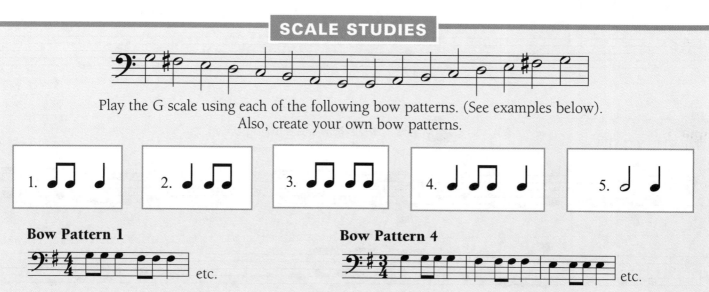

Play the G scale using each of the following bow patterns. (See examples below).
Also, create your own bow patterns.

1.   2.   3.   4.   5.

Bow Pattern 1

etc.

Bow Pattern 4

etc.

107 LA CLOCHE (Round)

French

108 OLD MACDONALD

North American

109 SWEET BETSY FROM PIKE

North American

110 FROGGIE GOES A' COURTIN'

North American

A

B

Switch parts on repeat.

A

B

Name the tetrachords, then write the tetrachords and the G Major scale.

G Down tetrachord   C Down tetrachord   G Major scale

SLUR DISCOVERY

111 SLUR PREPARATION 〰 = tap 1st finger freely

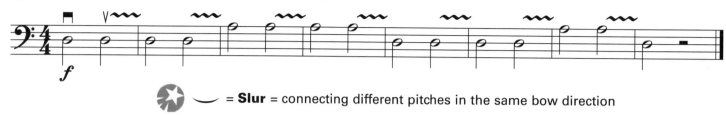

⭐ ⌣ = **Slur** = connecting different pitches in the same bow direction

112 G DOWN TETRACHORD SLURS

113 C DOWN TETRACHORD SLURS

114 SLUR MEETS THE G MAJOR SCALE

115 STARTING ON D

116 STARTING ON G

117 BUTTERSCOTCH WALTZ

String Crossing = moving the bow from one string to another

Bow Levels

← A String
← D String
← G String
← C String

STOPPED Slurs—Stop the bow after each note.

SMOOTH Slurs—Keep the bow moving!

118 STOPPED SLURS UP-DOWN

119 SMOOTH CROSSINGS UP-DOWN

120 ODE TO JOY (with slurs)—Memorize this piece and watch your bow!   Ludwig van Beethoven

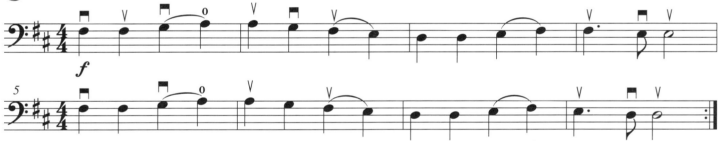

121 STOPPED SLURS COMBINATION

122 SMOOTH CROSSINGS COMBINATION

123 WAVY SLURS

SB303VC

More Bowing Styles

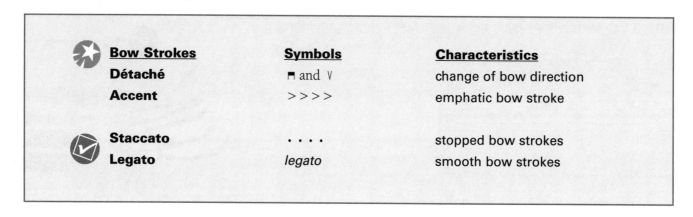

Bow Strokes	Symbols	Characteristics
Détaché	⊓ and ∨	change of bow direction
Accent	> > > >	emphatic bow stroke
Staccato	. . . .	stopped bow strokes
Legato	legato	smooth bow strokes

124 BOW STYLE STUDY—Play on each string.

125 THROUGH THE VALLEY

126 TWISTING

Write the bow stroke names on the blank spaces.

127 JIM ALONG JOSIE

North American

128 AURA LEE

Traditional

SB303VC

(129) PIECE PETITE—ensemble piece

Elliot Del Borgo

String Crossing Study—Play on D and A.

Upper String

Lower String   WB   UH   WB   LH   WB   UH   WB   LH

(130) LONG, LONG AGO

Traditional

Switch parts on repeat.

Learning About Ties

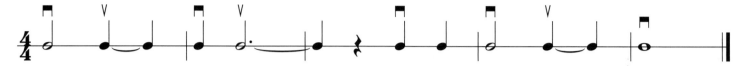

Bow Ties—Pay special attention to bow speed. Play on the D string.

Jean Sibelius (1865–1957) composed music that described the people and country of his native Finland. *Finlandia* is identified with Finland's movement for independence and national identity.

131 FINLANDIA—ensemble piece

Jean Sibelius

132 SHALOM CHAVERIM

Upbeat

Hebrew

Switch parts on repeat.

Circle the rhythm examples that are correct.

Chromatic = moving up or down by half steps

 SHARP
The sharp (♯) raises a note by ½ step.

 NATURAL
The natural (♮) cancels a sharp or flat.

 FLAT
The flat (♭) lowers a note by ½ step.

 Accidentals = sharp, natural, and flat symbols for altering pitch

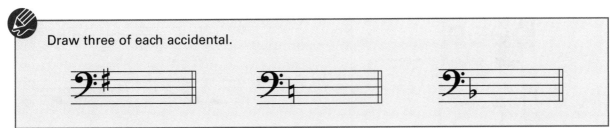

Draw three of each accidental.

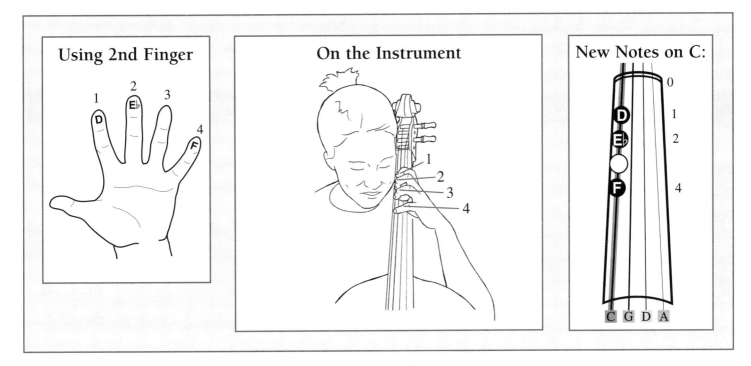

Using 2nd Finger

On the Instrument

New Notes on C:

For these studies: violins and basses on E, violas and cellos on C

Accidental Study One

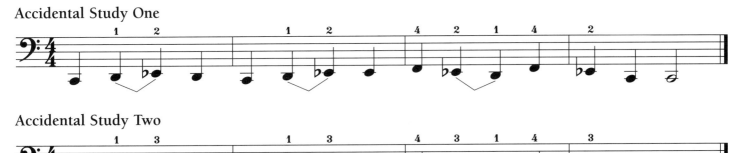

Accidental Study Two

Accidental Study Two

133 STRINGS HIGH AND LOW!

SB303VC

Accidentals on All Strings

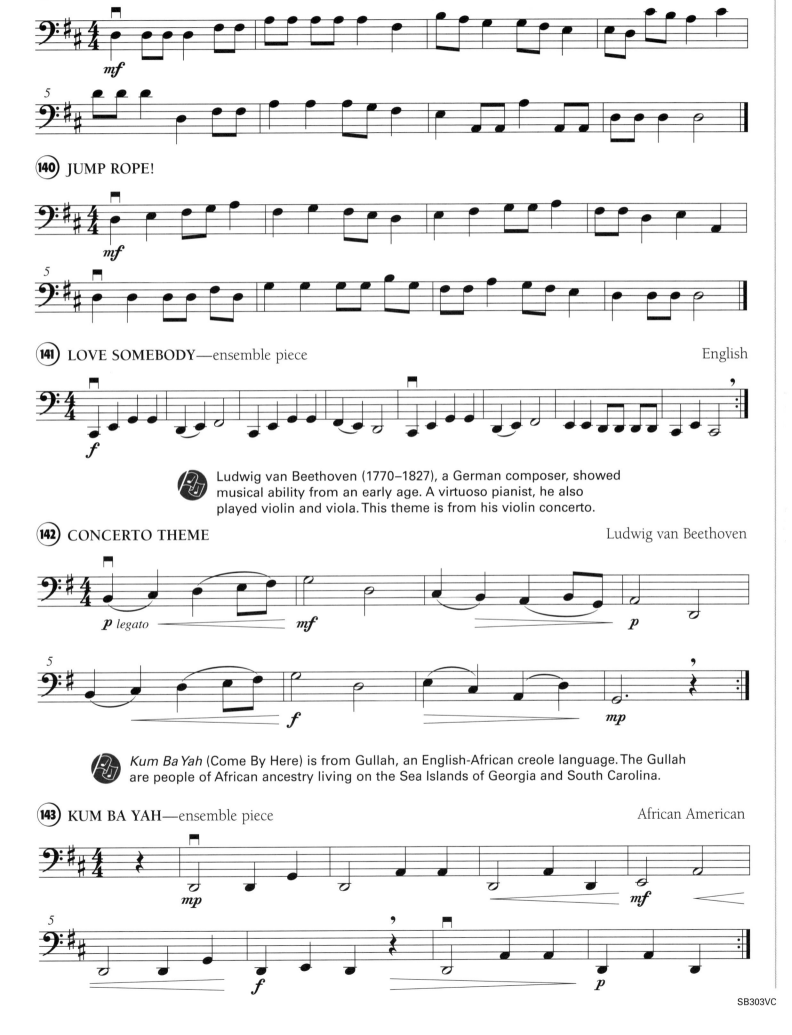

139 HOPSCOTCH!

140 JUMP ROPE!

141 LOVE SOMEBODY—ensemble piece

English

Ludwig van Beethoven (1770–1827), a German composer, showed musical ability from an early age. A virtuoso pianist, he also played violin and viola. This theme is from his violin concerto.

142 CONCERTO THEME

Ludwig van Beethoven

Kum Ba Yah (Come By Here) is from Gullah, an English-African creole language. The Gullah are people of African ancestry living on the Sea Islands of Georgia and South Carolina.

143 KUM BA YAH—ensemble piece

African American

144 CHROMATIC BOOGIE   **Chromatic**

145 BLUES ON ROUTE 259—Clap the A part rhythm pattern.

146 ACCIDENTAL BLUES—Find the A part repeated rhythms.

Yankee Doodle was written in the 1750s during the French and Indian War by British doctor Richard Shuckburg. Although the lyrics mocked the colonial Americans, they adopted the tune as their own.

(147) YANKEE DOODLE—ensemble piece (Memorize this piece.)

English

The kookaburra is an Australian bird, the world's largest kingfisher. The kookaburra's song (cry) sounds like a human laughing.

(148) KOOKABURRA SITS IN THE OLD GUM TREE (Round)

Marion Sinclair

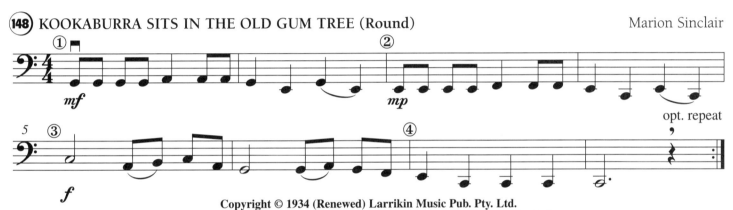

opt. repeat

My Country 'Tis of Thee is known in England as *God Save the King/Queen.* The earliest printed version of this tune dates to 1744; the earliest known performance was in 1745. In the United States, *My Country 'Tis of Thee* shared status as the national anthem with the *Star-Spangled Banner* until 1931, when the *Star-Spangled Banner* became the official national anthem.

(149) AMERICA (My Country 'Tis of Thee)

Lyrics: Samuel F. Smith
Music from Thesaurus Musicus

The upper C Down Tetrachord and the F Down Tetrachord

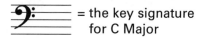

= the key signature for C Major

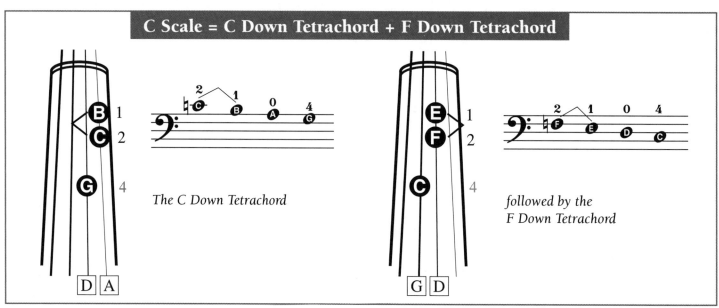

C Scale = C Down Tetrachord + F Down Tetrachord

The C Down Tetrachord

followed by the F Down Tetrachord

1. Sing   2. *Pizz.*   3. *Arco*

SCALE STUDIES

Play the C scale using each of the following bow patterns. (See examples below).
Also, create your own bow patterns.

1.   2.   3.   4.   5.

Bow Pattern 1   etc.   **Bow Pattern 2**   etc.   **Bow Pattern 4**   etc.

IMPROVISATION LOOP

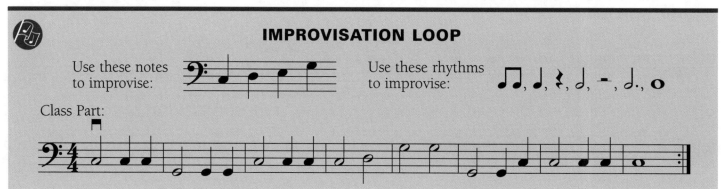

Use these notes to improvise:

Use these rhythms to improvise:

Class Part:

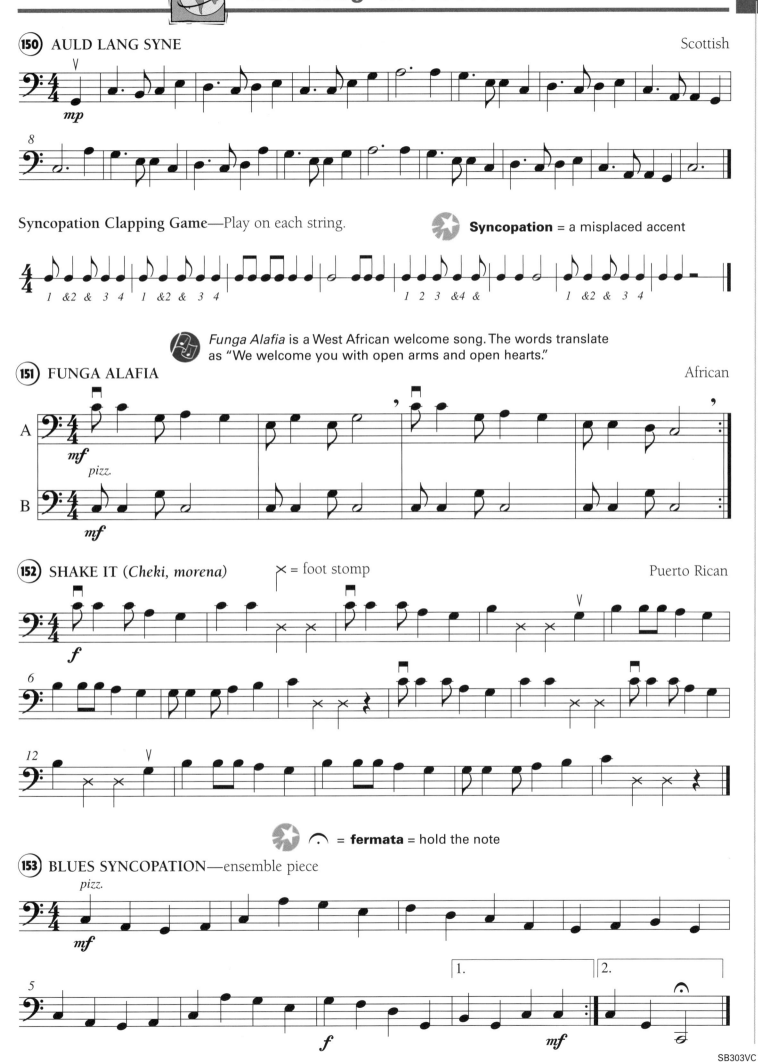

150 AULD LANG SYNE Scottish

Syncopation Clapping Game—Play on each string.

Syncopation = a misplaced accent

1 &2 & 3 4   1 &2 & 3 4   1 2 3 &4 &   1 &2 & 3 4

Funga Alafia is a West African welcome song. The words translate as "We welcome you with open arms and open hearts."

151 FUNGA ALAFIA African

152 SHAKE IT (Cheki, morena)   ✗ = foot stomp   Puerto Rican

⌢ = **fermata** = hold the note

153 BLUES SYNCOPATION—ensemble piece

SB303VC

154 MI GALLO (Round)

Mexican

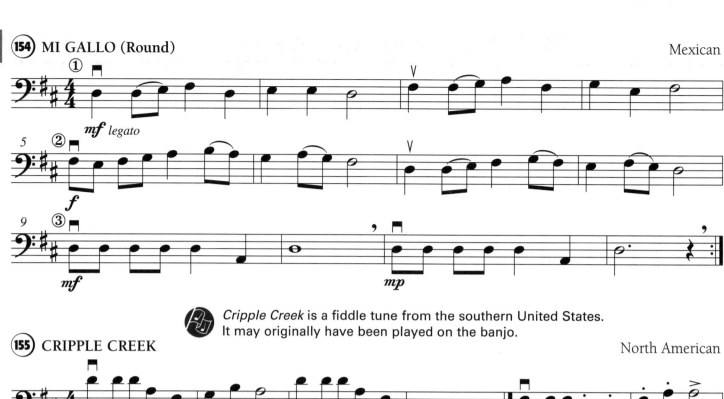

Cripple Creek is a fiddle tune from the southern United States. It may originally have been played on the banjo.

155 CRIPPLE CREEK

North American

The minuet is a graceful dance in a meter of three. This minuet was written by J.S. Bach (1685–1750) for the *Harpsichord Suite in g minor*. Bach was a composer and organist from a very musical German family.

156 MINUET NO. 1

Johann Sebastian Bach

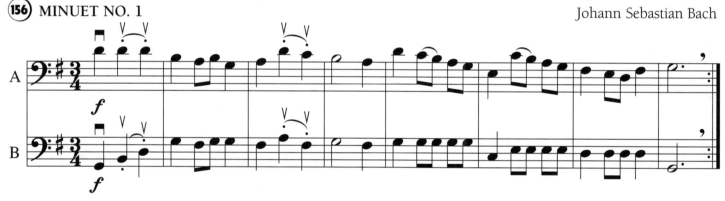

Gioachino Rossini (1792–1868) was an Italian composer. Very famous in his own time, he played viola, French horn, and sang. His opera, *William Tell,* was first performed in 1829.

157 WILLIAM TELL—*ensemble piece*

Gioachino Rossini

Double Stop March

 Double stop = playing two strings at the same time

Moderato (♩ = 104)

Elliot Del Borgo

Bagpipes and Kilts

Soon Hee Newbold

Rock-on Strings

Soon Hee Newbold

ADVANCED TECHNIQUES

 Arpeggio = notes of a chord played separately

D Major Scale and Arpeggio

161 CALISTHENICS IN D

162 ADVANCED MUSICIANSHIP STUDY IN D

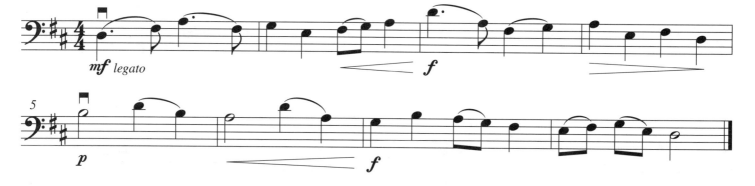

G Major Scale and Arpeggio

163 CALISTHENICS IN G

164 ADVANCED MUSICIANSHIP STUDY IN G

C Major Scale and Arpeggio

165 CALISTHENICS IN C

166 ADVANCED MUSICIANSHIP STUDY IN C

Solo Performance

Memorize One of These Solos

171 March in G

179 Piano Accompaniment Only

Johann Sebastian Bach
arranged by Joanne Erwin

Allegro (♩ = 104)

Johannes Brahms (1833–1897), a German composer, studied cello, piano, and French horn in his youth. He composed large works such as symphonies, as well as chamber music, piano pieces, songs, and choral music. Brahms, J.S. Bach, and Beethoven are known as the "Three B's" of music.

(172) THEME FROM SYMPHONY NO. 1

(180) Piano Accompaniment Only

Johannes Brahms
arranged by Joanne Erwin

Moderato (♩ = 108)

Accent (>) emphatic bow strokes.

Accidentals (♯, ♮, ♭) sharp, natural, and flat symbols for altering pitch.

Arco to play using the bow.

Arpeggio notes of a chord played separately.

Beat the pulse of the music.

Bow lanes point of contact of the bow, near the bridge or near the fingerboard.

Chromatic moving up or down by half steps.

Clef sign (𝄢) located at the beginning of each line of music, the clef sign defines the letter names for the lines and spaces on the staff for your instrument.

Crescendo (——————) gradually playing louder.

Détaché change of bow direction.

Diminuendo (——————) gradually playing softer.

Double stop playing two strings at the same time.

Down bow (⊓) moving bow toward tip.

Duet music in two parts.

Dynamics symbols indicating how loudly or softly to play.

Fermata (⌢) symbol indicating to hold a note longer.

First ending (𝄆) play this ending the first time through a piece.

Flat (♭) lowers a pitch by ½ step.

Forte (𝆑) play loudly, with a full sound.

Harmony pitches that accompany the melody or tune.

Improvise creating music spontaneously without using written notes.

Key signature identifies notes that are raised or lowered.

Ledger lines (☰) extend the staff with small lines written above or below.

Legato play with smooth bow strokes.

Maestoso majestically.

Measure (▭) the space between barlines.

Melody main tune.

Mezzo medium, as in 𝒎𝒇 medium loud, 𝒎𝒑 medium soft.

Natural (♮) cancels out a sharp or flat that is in the key signature, or a preceding sharp or flat in a measure.

Octave pitch that is eight notes higher or lower and has the same letter name.

Piano (𝒑) play softly.

Pizzicato (*pizz.*) pluck the string with the index finger of the right hand. (+) = pluck the string with the left hand.

Repeat sign (𝄇) go back and play a section of music again.

Retake (') lift the bow from the string and return to the frog in a circular motion.

Ritardando (*rit.*) gradually getting slower.

Round the same music starting at different times.

Scale tetrachord + tetrachord. A scale begins and ends on the same letter name.

Second ending (𝄆) play this ending the second time.

Sharp (♯) raises a pitch by ½ step.

Slur (⌒) connecting different pitches on the same bow direction.

Staccato (·) stopped bow stroke.

Staff (☰) 5 lines and 4 spaces, used for writing music.

Syncopation misplaced accent; emphasis is placed "off" the beat.

Tetrachord 4-note pattern of pitches that occurs in alphabetical order (up and down). For example, D-E-F♯-G, G-F♯-E-D.

Theme melody.

Tie marking that connects notes of the same pitch together without a break.

Time signature indicates how many beats are in a measure (top number) and what kind of note gets one beat (bottom number).

Up bow (⋁) moving bow toward frog.

Upbeat note(s) that appear before the first barline. The upbeat is subtracted from the last measure of music.

Variation altered melody.